My Santa, Your Santa

WRITTEN BY
Margaret Thompson

ILLUSTRATED BY
Roger Weaver

To Zander,
This book wouldn't exist without you.
Love you to the moon and back,
Mum and Dad

Special thanks to Rafi and Mike

Library of Congress Cataloging-in-Publication Data

Thompson, Margaret, 2020

Library of Congress Control Number: 2020921254

ISBN: 9798681929734

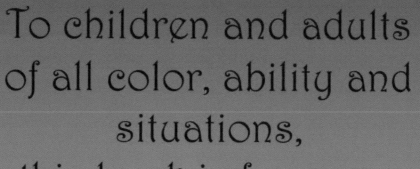

To children and adults
of all color, ability and
situations,
this book is for you...
because Santa is for
everyone.

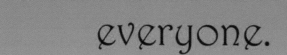

He might look like you or me,

or anyone in our family.

Santa's sack is filled with
gifts and toys,
For all the good little girls and boys.

Your gift might be red, green or blue.
What did your Santa give to you?

My Santa gave me

_____

#mysantayoursanta

Printed in Great Britain
by Amazon